T1l

God's Answers for Today

Rachel Hall-Smith

'Pray as you talk' network

Praying to God can be like chatting to a friend on your mobile phone (only easier - no bills to pay, no RNA). You can call at any time and God is eager to receive your messages! Ephesians 6:18 says, "Pray... on all occasions with all kind of prayers and requests." So we can tell God about anything that concerns or puzzles us. We know that God hears us and will encourage and help us(Psalm 34:17.) This book uses text messages to ask God a number of questions. "Text chat", abbreviations and symbols, are at the back of the book.

"Tlk 2 GOD"

Dear God... how do I know if the Bible is true? It could be just an old myth, written hundreds of years ago. :-\

Dear Friend… my Word, the Bible, HAS been around for a long time, but is STILL the best thing to read to show you how to get the MOST out of YOUR LIFE, TODAY! It is STILL the World's Number 1 best seller! Although many different people wrote the Bible books, I inspired and guided them all. (2 Timothy 3:16) FYI In it I teach you about myself, faith, and life. And through it I CAN SPEAK TO YOU TODAY. Read it and see! TLK2U L8R

"Tlk 2 GOD"

BTW ... Lots of things in life are uncertain, but my word the Bible teaches solid truths which you can base your life upon. It gives you 'absolutes', i.e. what is right and what is wrong. The Bible says *"Therefore everyone who hears these words of mine and puts them into practice is like a wise man who built his house on the rock. The rain came down, the streams rose and the winds blew and beat against that house; yet it did not fall, because it had its foundation on the rock." (Matthew 7:24-25)* IOW if you put my advice into practice, you will know security and your life will not fall "with a great crash." (v27) HTH.

AYT, God? WAN2TLK?

"Tlk 2 GOD"

Yes I am and Yes I do. I have always been here. *John 1:1-2 "In the beginning was the Word, and the Word was with God, and the Word was God. He was with God in the beginning."*

But how can I know UR real? I can't see you! — Q

You can't see electricity but you know it's real. You see its effects. In the same way, you can see MY effects, e.g. In the beauty of creation, in the lives of Christians. Ask me to become "real" to you. I have promised... *"Ask and it will be given to you; seek and you will find; knock and the door will be opened to you." (Matthew 7:7)* There will NEVER be a RNA! I hear you and respond to you. *"Ask and you will receive and your joy will be complete." John 16:24.*

5

"Tlk 2 GOD"

This does NOT mean that you should come to me with a shopping list of THINGS you want and that I will supply them! That would be asking with wrong motives. *"When you ask you do not receive because you ask with wrong motives, that you may spend what you get on your own pleasures." (James 4:3).* I want what is best for you. That may be different from what you ask me! So, sometimes I will say "Yes," or "No" or "Wait." *"If you then, though you are evil, know how to give good gifts to your children, how much more will your father in heaven give good gifts to those who ask him." (Matthew 7:11)*
HTH

"Tlk 2 GOD"

So, how do I know WHAT to pray?

This is a FAQ. For starters, you should use these guidelines TNX/SRY/PLS.

TNX – praise me for who I am and all I have done for you.

SRY – admit the wrong you have done, ask me to forgive and turn you from your old ways.

PLS – pray for friends, family, yourself, people in need – as you feel in your heart. Read Luke chapter 11 to see how Jesus taught you to pray.

"Tlk 2 GOD"

Dear God — how do I know if I'm forgiven? MY HEART FEELS SO BLACK! I try to be good but I've done so many wrong things and I can't seem to do what's right! PCB :-(

Dear Friend…I am a God of justice and holiness but I have promised that I WILL forgive you! My word, the Bible, says so. *"If we confess our sins, he is faithful and just and will forgive us our sins and purify us from all unrighteousness." (1 John 1:9)* IOW… if you say you are sorry and really mean it, I will TURN YOUR HEART from BLACK TO WHITE! A fresh start! (Isaiah 1:18)

"Tlk 2 GOD"

Attn... ILUVU so much, that I sent my Son Jesus Christ, to earth. He died in YOUR place. *But God shows his own love for us in this way: "While we were still sinners Christ died for us. "(Romans 5:8)* Jesus died in your place so that you can be forgiven. This is my promise: *"He who conceals his sins does not prosper, but whoever confesses and renounces them finds mercy."* *(Proverbs 28:13)* IOW... when you say SRY turn your back on wrong and ask my Son Jesus in to your heart, you will be saved! You can change from :- (to this +:-) Praise the Lord! \o/ *"I tell you, there is rejoicing in the presence of the angels of God over one sinner who repents." (Luke 15:10)*

"Tlk 2 GOD"

But IDGI. If he was SO powerful, why was he put to death? :-\ :-Q

AISB, I am a God of justice and holiness and *"the wages of sin is death." (Romans 6:23)* Because of your sin you deserve death. Jesus had to take this punishment so that YOU could be saved and be clothed in his righteousness. IOW if you don't trust in My Son then all I see is your sin. But if you do trust him, instead of seeing your sin I see my perfect, righteous Son. This is because of what he did on the cross. He gave his life for YOU. He took YOUR punishment! He took away YOUR sin. *"This is love: not that we loved God, but that he loved us and sent his Son as an atoning sacrifice for our sins."* (1 John 4:10) TLK2U L8R

"Tlk 2 GOD"

/o\ Heavenly Father what can I say? TNX for your love which sent JESUS to die in my place. I am SRY for the wrong things I have done. PLS forgive me and may JESUS come into my heart. HLP me to live the right way, as I want to be a Christian +:-) and serve you. LOL

My child, as I have loved you, live in my love *"Love the Lord your God with all your heart and with all your soul and with all your mind. This is the first and greatest commandment."* (Matthew 22:37-38) *"And the second is like it ... Love your neighbour as yourself."* (Matthew 22:39) *"All men will know that you are my disciples if you love one another."* (John 13:35) :->>> KIT

11

"Tlk 2 GOD"

:-[Dear God — if I tell a lie, even a small one, why does it make me feel so bad? PCB :-Q :'-(

Dear friend – when you become a Christian, I make you a *"new creation" (2 Corinthians 5:17) and my Holy Spirit comes to live inside you. (Romans 8:9)* The Holy Spirit convicts you when you return to your old nature. I am a God of light and truth, not darkness and lies (1 John 1:5 and Hebrews 6:18) and so those *"controlled by the sinful nature cannot please God." (Romans 8:8)* BUT FYI the good news is *"if by the Spirit you put to death the misdeeds of the body, you will live." (Romans 8:13) so confess your sins, and I will forgive you, and you can start afresh! (1 John 1:9)*

"Tlk 2 GOD"

But I try to stop lying/swearing. It's hard when everyone else is doing it!

Attn… There is a spiritual battle going on – the forces of God/good against the forces of the Devil/evil. (Ephesians 6:12) Do two things - DEFEND and ATTACK. DEFENCE: In Ephesians 6:11-18 the Bible tells you how to put on "the full armour of God." This involves growing in righteousness by using the Word of God. ATTACK: Pray for my strength (Ephesians 6:18). Use the words of Psalm 19:14 *"May the words of my mouth and the meditation of my heart be acceptable in your sight, O Lord, my strength and redeemer."* TAKE A STAND. When a wrong thought comes into your mind, throw it out immediately! (2 Corinthians 10:5) AISB The Holy Spirit will give you power to choose to do what is right. (Acts 1:8) KUTGW.

"Peer Tlk"

F2T? I want a pair of new designer trainers! Everyone has them but Mum said we can't afford them. I prayed about it but when I tried to change Mum's mind, she grounded me! PCB

:-O FYI: This thing with your mum is NAGI. BYKT and BTW don't use prayer to get your own way! God likes you to have nice gifts (1 Timothy 6:17) but

a) The Bible says, *"Obey your parents in the Lord for this is right. Honour your father and mother ... that it may go well with you and that you may enjoy long life on the earth." (Ephesians 6:1-3)*

b) Christians should show PATIENCE and SELF CONTROL (Galatians 5:22-23) and Paul speaks about the importance of "being CONTENT". (1 Timothy 6:8)

"Peer Tlk"

c) Think of things from your mum's point of view. When money is tight, she has to decide on priorities. WTTW – spend some, save some and give some to the Lord. (Malachi 3:10)

d) It can be nice to wear designer gear like your friends, but don't let it become your major priority. *"The Lord does not look at the things man looks at. Man looks at the outward appearance, but the Lord looks at the heart." (1 Samuel 16:7)* TTFN.

```
Okay. I'll go and say "Sry" to Mum
and I'll TRY to change my attitude
to show that I mean it!  But AISB
I would STILL like those trainers!
BBFN ;- )
```

15

"Tlk 2 GOD"

Dear God — Why can kids at school be so nasty to me? They say such horrible things! HLP :-(

Dear friend – People who do not know me as their Father can experience a lot of unhappiness. This does NOT excuse their behaviour but HTH you to see what is behind their unkind words and actions. The Bible says a) *"A gentle answer turns away wrath, but a harsh word stirs up anger." (Proverbs 15:1)* b) *"Do not say, 'I'll pay you back for this wrong!' Wait for the Lord and he will deliver you." (Proverbs 20:22)* IOW Do NOT retaliate! c) *"PRAY for those who persecute you." (Matthew 5:44)* d) *"Be kind and compassionate to one another forgiving each other, just as in Christ God forgave you." (Ephesians 4:32)* Attn The Bible warns… *"For if you forgive men*

"Tlk 2 GOD"

when they sin against you, your heavenly Father will also forgive you. But if you do not forgive men their sins, your Father will not forgive your sins." (Matthew 6:14-15)

```
WDYMBT? It's not so easy to forgive! I
resent them when they try and stop
others from being my friend. :-(
```

Dear Friend, No – it is NOT easy. But pray about it and ask for my wisdom. It may be worth re-assessing your friendships. Proverbs 12:26 says "The righteous should choose his friends carefully, for the way of the wicked leads them astray." Seek positive friendships with those who show kindness and loyalty.

"Peer Tlk"

F2T? I'm being bullied! What should I do? :'-(Someone deliberately tripped me over in the playground and his friends chucked my bag around. PLS HLP :-(

HTH. Physical violence or excessive taunting is BULLYING and this is a serious matter. You need to tell someone you trust – a family member or a teacher you can speak to. Schools have 'anti-bullying policies' and it is important to report bullying as it should not happen. In addition to seeking support from your family or a teacher, remember that God is One who will NEVER fail you. PCB

"Tlk 2 GOD"

Dear God... how do I know what I should do with my life? I'll have LOTS of decisions to make — what to study at school, which job to train for, whether I should marry, etc. How do I know what is best for me? :-Q

Dear friend. Don't worry — you won't have to make these decisions on your own! I have given you your family or adults that you respect at school and church. They will be happy to support you and give you advice. And, most importantly… *"I will instruct you and teach you in the way you should go; I will counsel you and watch over you." (Psalm 32:8)*

"Tlk 2 GOD"

The people who wrote the Psalms in the Bible found their confidence in me – *"The Lord is my light and my salvation. He is the strength of my life. Of whom shall I be afraid?" Psalm 27:1 "I will lie down and sleep in peace; for you alone, O Lord, make me dwell in safety." Psalm 4:8*

```
IDGI. How can you show me what to do? The
Bible doesn't tell me to take History
instead of Geography or to train as a
Doctor and not a Nurse! :-\
```

But my Word DOES give good advice for living. Ask ME for advice and I will show you the way ahead. I am "not a God of disorder but of peace." (1 Corinthians 14:33) IOW – you will know peace in your heart when you take the correct action. AISB: seek advice from those you respect and use your common sense.

"Tlk 2 GOD"

But God — what if I make a mistake and choose the wrong thing :- (?

I can help if you trust in me. You don't have to do what your friends do. Romans 12:2 says *"Do not conform to the pattern of this world (IOW – peer pressure) but renew your mind (IOW – see things from God's point of view).* Then you will discover God's good and perfect will." BTW - I have your life *"in the palm of my hands" (Isaiah 49:16)* and *"I know the plans I have for you ... plans to prosper you and not to harm you, plans to give you hope and a future'." (Jeremiah 29:11)* :- >> TLK2U L8R

"Tlk 2 GOD"

Dear God — Can you be a Christian without going to Church?

Dear friend — Going to Church each Sunday doesn't make you a Christian, but it is an important thing for Christians to do. Paul says... *"Let us not give up meeting together... but let us ENCOURAGE ONE ANOTHER."* (Hebrews 10:25) As you... *"devote yourself to the public reading of the Scripture... and teaching."* (1 Timothy 4:13) you will GROW SPIRITUALLY. Christians are like... *"the body of Christ, and each one of you is a part of it."* (1 Corinthians 12:27) If one of the parts of the body is absent, the body as a whole can't function properly. TLK2U L8R

"Peer Tlk"

F2T? How do I know which Church to attend? :-\

HTH. There are differences between Churches, as there are differences between people. Styles of worship and certain beliefs vary. However, it is ESSENTIAL to find a Church which recognises JESUS as Lord and the CROSS as your means of SALVATION. IOW they must believe that the only way to heaven is through trusting in the Lord Jesus Christ and in his death on the cross to save us from our sins. He then rose again from the dead! :->>>You were created to Worship \o/ \o/ \o/, and God wants you to share your faith with others. The Bible says *"Make disciples of all nations." Matthew 28:19* Remember this when deciding which Church Family to join. SIT. BCNU

"Peer Tlk"

F2T? My ears stick out my hair's too curly. And I've got ANOTHER spot! No one will ever fancy me looking like this. What do I do? :- '(

HUH - Your spots will go, especially if you eat healthily, drink plenty water and exercise! Make the most of yourself! Spend time with friends and don't get stressed about the boyfriend/girlfriend thing. Trust God, who is a friend who sticks closer than the best brother. Spend time with him too! The Bible says *"Do not conform... to the pattern of this world." (Romans 12:2). "Charm is deceptive and beauty is fleeting." (Proverbs 31:30)* HTH: True joy and peace comes from knowing God's LUV4U, your creator, your saviour. Ask him into your heart and the beauty and attractiveness that he brings will radiate out from you.

"Peer Tlk"

"Your body is a temple of the Holy Spirit, who is in you… therefore honour God with your body." (1 Corinthians 6:19-20) WTTW… *"Whoever of you loves life and desires to see many good days" (Psalm 34:12)* should turn to God's Word to find the BEST rules for living!

F2T? Why am I useless at EVERYTHING! :-(

UR NOT useless at everything! God says: *"I made you in my image" (Genesis 1:26)*. UR unique – and *"Each one has his own gift from God, one has this gift another has that." (1 Corinthians 7:7)* IOW- EACH person has things they are good at. You just need to find your "thing"! There may be something, which you have not yet tried, which you could excel at! In Exodus 4, Moses didn't want

"Peer Tlk"

God to make him a leader as he didn't think he was good at speaking. But God promised *"I will help you speak and will teach you what to say", (verse12)* and Moses succeeded in his task. The New Testament apostles found their strength in God too – *"I can do everything through him who gives me strength." (Philippians 4:13)* TLK2U L8R? STSP?

F2T? Can anybody help? I want to look great like the popstars on TV! They are popular and earn loads of money.

"Peer Tlk"

URSPSHL just the way you are! God says: *I knit you together in your Mum's womb. (Psalm 139:13)* You only have to read the Bible to see JUST HOW MUCH God loves you. *"For God loved the world so much that he sent his only son that whoever believes in him will not perish but live for ever. " (John 3:16)* It's NAGI to think that the popstars are the 'ideal' to strive towards. They might APPEAR successful but they often portray the wrong ideals. You cannot find TRUE happiness in beauty, fame, or money either!

```
TNX! But WDYMBT? I'm struggling at
school. I need to pass my exams if I
want a good job! Don't tell me to
ask the teacher for help. I did, but
I ended up copying my friends anyway!
```

27

"Peer Tlk"

WTTW. You can get HLP from
a) Your teachers (I know you said not to advise this!)
b) HLP outside school
c) HLP from God.
d) HLP yourself!

a)   Instead of asking the teacher in front of your classmates, go and see him/her after the lesson. Their job is to help you and they should be pleased that UR showing initiative!

b)   It is possible to get 'study guides', HLP 0n-line via the Internet, or from another teacher.

c)   In Exodus 4, Moses didn't want God to make him a leader as he didn't think he was good at speaking (verse 10). But this is what God promised... *"I will help you speak and will teach you what to say,"* (v12) and Moses

"Peer Tlk"

succeeded. The New Testament apostles found their strength in God too – *"I can do everything through him who gives me strength."* (Philippians 4:13)

d) You need to discipline yourself to persevere even when the going gets tough! (BYKT!) Proverbs 14:23 says… *"All hard work brings a profit,"* so commitment pays off!

```
TNX. That's GR8. I'll give it
another go!
;- )
```

KUTGW !! :-)

KEY TO "TEXT CHAT"
AISB: as I said before
ATTN: Attention
AYT: are you there?
BCNU: be seeing you
BTW: by the way
BYKT: but you knew that
FAQ: frequently asked questions
FYI: for your information
F2T: Free to talk
GR8: Great
HTH: hope this helps
HUH: have you heard?
HLP: Help
IDGI: I don't get it
ILUVU: I love you
IOW: in other words
KIT: keep in touch
KUTGW: keep up the good work
LUV4U: Love for you
LOL: Lot's of love
M4U: message for you
NAGI: not a good idea
PCB: please call back
Pls: please
RNA: ring no answer
SIT: STAY IN TOUCH
Sry: sorry!
STSP: Same time same place
TLK2U L8R: Talk to you later
TNX: THANKS!
TTFN: TA TA FOR NOW
UR: YOU ARE
URSPSHL: You are special
WAN2TLK: WANT TO TALK?
WDYMBT: WHAT Do you mean by that?
WTTW: Word to the wise

SIDEWAYS FACES TO SHOW HOW YOU ARE FEELING

\o/   Praise the Lord
/o\   Person praying
:- (sad, disappointed face
:- '(sad, with spot!
:-[down, unhappy
:'-(I am crying!
:-\   confused, undecided
:-0   surprised, shocked
:-Q   I don't understand
;-)   Joking, happy
:-))   very happy

:->>   a huge smile
:->>>   overjoyed face!
+:-)   a Christian

Tlk 2 Me Answers for Today copyright 2003 Rachel Hall-Smith
Published by Christian Focus Publications, Geanies House,
Fearn, Tain, Ross-shire, IV20 1TW, Scotland, UK.
www.christianfocus.com
All rights reserved. No part of this publication may be
reproduced, stored in a retrieval system, or transmitted, in
any form, by any means, electronic, mechanical, photocopying,
recording or otherwise without the prior permission of the
publisher or a license permitting restricted copying. In the
U.K. such licenses are issued by the Copyright Licensing
Agency, 90 Tottenham Court Road, London W1P 9HE.
Artwork: Jonathan Williams Cover Design: Alister Macinnes

M4U
"Do not be anxious about anything, but in everything, by prayer
and petition, with thanksgiving, present your requests to God.
And the peace of God, which transcends all understanding, will
guard you hearts and your minds in Christ Jesus."
(Philippians 4:6-7)